# YEAR 4

# MODE, MEDIAN, MEAN, RANGE

# Numbers up to 10

Name: _____

Class: _____

Date: _____

This book is dedicated to all those seeking knowledge.

## *THE PEN IS MIGHTIER THAN THE SWORD*

Edward Nulwer-Lytton (1839)

# Contents

Title Page ................................................................................ 1

Contents and Progress Chart ..................................................... 7

**Exercises** ............................................................................. 11

    Exercise 1: Five Numbers

    Exercise 2: Seven Numbers

    Exercise 3: Nine Numbers

Answer Sheet ......................................................................... 25

# Progress Chart

| Exercises | Page | Test A | Test B |
|---|---|---|---|
| Exercise 1 : Five Numbers | 11 | /12 | /12 |
| Exercise 2: Seven Numbers | 15 | /12 | /12 |
| Exercise 3: Nine Numbers | 19 | /12 | /12 |

## EXERCISE 1: Five Numbers

### Test A

1.     3    8    3    5    10

What is the mode?          _____

What is the median?        _____

What is the mean?          _____

What is the range?         _____


2.     7    6    6    10    1

What is the mode?          _____

What is the median?        _____

What is the mean?          _____

What is the range?         _____


3.     9    10    0    8    0

What is the mode?          _____

What is the median?        _____

What is the mean?          _____

What is the range?         _____

Score:        /12

Prep4YourExams.com

**Test B**

1.     4     7     7     9     8

    What is the range?         _____

    What is the mean?          _____

    What is the median?        _____

    What is the mode?          _____


2.     2     8     9     2     1

    What is the mean?          _____

    What is the mode?          _____

    What is the range?         _____

    What is the median?        _____


3.     9     0     2     3     3

    What is the median?        _____

    What is the mean?          _____

    What is the range?         _____

    What is the mode?          _____

**Score:**        /12

## EXERCISE 2: Seven Numbers

### Test A

1.     1    7    0    2    1    1    6

What is the mode?      _____

What is the median?    _____

What is the mean?      _____

What is the range?     _____

2.     8    4    1    2    6    3    6

What is the mode?      _____

What is the median?    _____

What is the mean?      _____

What is the range?     _____

3.     9    3    8    3    1    6    2

What is the mode?      _____

What is the median?    _____

What is the mean?      _____

What is the range?     _____

Score:        /12

**Test B**

1.  2   5   1   5   8   6   10

    What is the range?      _____

    What is the mean?       _____

    What is the median?     _____

    What is the mode?       _____


2.  2   4   6   6   4   6   8

    What is the mean?       _____

    What is the mode?       _____

    What is the range?      _____

    What is the median?     _____


3.  2   3   2   9   8   5   6

    What is the median?     _____

    What is the mean?       _____

    What is the range?      _____

    What is the mode?       _____

**Score:**      **/12**

## EXERCISE 3: Nine Numbers

### Test A

1.     4     9     4     9     3     0     6     6     6

What is the mode?     _____

What is the median?     _____

What is the mean?     _____

What is the range?     _____

2.     4     8     4     5     8     5     5     6     6

What is the mode?     _____

What is the median?     _____

What is the mean?     _____

What is the range?     _____

3.     9     9     4     6     10     10     0     9     1

What is the mode?     _____

What is the median?     _____

What is the mean?     _____

What is the range?     _____

Score:     /12

**Test B**

1.     6    8    9    8    2    3    2    1    0

What is the range?     _____

What is the mean?      _____

What is the median?    _____

What is the mode?      _____

2.     1    3    9    2    3    8    5    5    5

What is the mean?      _____

What is the mode?      _____

What is the range?     _____

What is the median?    _____

3.     3    4    4    9    7    4    6    5    7

What is the median?    _____

What is the mean?      _____

What is the range?     _____

What is the mode?      _____

Score:    /12

# Answers

**Ex 1 : Test A**

1.  mode = 5
    median = 5
    mean = 5.8
    range = 7

2.  mode = 6
    median = 6
    mean = 6
    range = 9

3.  mode = 0
    median = 8
    mean = 5.4
    range 10

**Ex 2 : Test A**

1.  mode = 1
    median = 1
    mean = 2.6
    range = 6

2.  mode = 6
    median = 4
    mean = 4.3
    range = 7

3.  mode = 3
    median = 3
    mean = 4.6
    range 8

**Ex 3 : Test A**

1.  mode = 6
    median = 6
    mean = 5.2
    range = 9

2.  mode = 5
    median = 5
    mean = 5.7
    range = 4

3.  mode = 9
    median = 9
    mean = 6.4
    range 10

**Test B**

1.  range = 5
    mean = 7
    median = 7
    mode = 7

2.  mean = 4.4
    mode = 2
    range = 7
    median = 2

3.  median = 3
    mean = 3.4
    range = 9
    mode = 3

**Test B**

1.  range = 9
    mean = 5.3
    median = 5
    mode = 5

2.  mean = 5.1
    mode = 6
    range = 6
    median = 6

3.  median = 5
    mean = 5
    range = 7
    mode = 2

**Test B**

1.  range = 9
    mean = 4.3
    median = 3
    mode = 2 & 8

2.  mean = 4.6
    mode = 5
    range = 8
    median = 5

3.  median = 5
    mean = 5.4
    range = 6
    mode = 4